FOREIGN HOMES

FOREIGN HOMES

JOAN CRATE

Brick Books

National Library of Canada Cataloguing in Publication Data

Crate, Joan, 1953–
    Foreign homes

Poems.
ISBN 1-894078-19-5

    1. Title

PS8555.R338F67 2001   C811'54   C2001-902944-6
PR9199.3.C66828F67 2001

We acknowledge the support of the Canada Council for the Arts for our publishing programme. The support of the Ontario Arts Council is also gratefully acknowledged.

The cover photograph of the author's in-laws and their family was taken by an unknown photographer around 1963 in Lebanon. Because divorce is illegal for Christians in Lebanon, the adults in the picture were legally married to other people and had been charged with adultery. It was hoped that a photograph of them with their children would persuade authorities to drop the charges. However, the picture failed to raise sympathy and they were both jailed, leaving their fourteen-year-old son (upper left) to look after the family. Their sentence was commuted within the year, in response to an appeal by Nasser to the president of Lebanon. The original photograph is from the author's personal collection.

The author photo is by Elaire Frenette.

Some of these poems have appeared in *Arc*, *Dandelion*, *Grain*, *Orbis* (U.K.), *Poetry Canada*, and *subTerrain*.

This book is set in Janson Text and Trump Mediaeval.

Design and layout by Alan Siu.
Printed and bound by Sunville Printco Inc.

Brick Books
431 Boler Road, Box 20081
London, Ontario   N6K 4G6

brick.books@sympatico.ca

This book is for Kamal

Contents

Dowries

Loose Feathers on Stone

Thieves

Dowries

Dowries

We have crossed borders to reach
each other and lost land
chafes our touch. I carry
snowshoes, winter wheat, raven call,
winter pocked by arsenic flakes from the mines.
You bring donkey sweat and spent bullets,
voices that shriek out, tear bright.

We offer them to each other—
gift and sacrifice.

My Grandfather Dreams

Wind rattles prairie ribs.
Flesh of cattle shrivels—
paper in flame. My grandfather swims
through a hot sea of wheat, honeyed waves
crush his dreams. He sobs in his sleep—
oh treacherous fantasy, calls
my grandmother but her name cracks
his lips. *Woman!*
She fades.

At noon he finds her making soup from tumbleweeds,
nettles in her tongue, her voice
gone to moan. Only
the roar of heat in his ears.

Once the juice of saskatoons smeared
her cheeks, her mouth ran with it,
womb full. Now she rattles
like a baby's outgrown toy.
He reaches for her, feels the past
melt in laughter, their bodies warm
pools, pulls back, afraid
of the black absences
he will leave
on her skin.
And so

he waits for her to swim backwards
to the landscape she came from—
northern trees and wet-lipped lakes.
The sky settles on his shoulders,
wind blasts every kernel of desire.
Is it *Delores? Dorothy?*
He sinks down in the dust.
She stands over him. Sun
burns to a cinder, all but
blinds him. *Darling—*
his last horizon.

Flight

My mother still has it,
a ceramic bird, plucked years ago
from a box of Nabob tea bags.
Not being one to throw things out,
not one to collect them either,
she dropped it on a kitchen shelf.

In the fire this sales gimmick flew.
Frantic bird-brain lifted wings over
burning books, tables, chairs,
photographs curling, screaming
cat crouched, ready to pounce,
orange and red claws flicking, oh never
                                    to land.

Outside my mother staggered through ruin—
their trailer in flames and no insurance.
My father came home from work
to find her calling, calling the cat.

Next day, searching for bones,
she reached into a nest of charcoal,
found the bird, eyes blackened
by visions of heaven and hell.
                    To think this alone
                    came through that fire.
                    A different shade. So much nicer,
my mother chirps as she serves tea
in cups donated by neighbours.
Her words lilt over the crackle of sugar,
quench of cream. She places the ceramic bird
on the second-hand dresser
in the basement suite they rent in town,
sits across from me, watching
my cramped face.
                    Things. Just things,
and I watch this old woman rise,
flit about the kitchen, searching
for a spoon.

Yellow flowers

I

dance my front lawn.
Knot them tight, a crown for my princess hair.

Insects bolt through grass blades.
I roll over them—somersaults, cartwheels. Whips
of brown hair ribbon green, yellow, blue.

Pick the legs off the daddy-longlegs
he loves me
he loves me not
The promise of you sleeps in my brain
like a tumour.

II

Dandelions
knot my lungs, my hair
whirs white wires—
horizontal lines through an unfocused life.

Adjust this picture,
rewrite the role,
kiss me awake—

small round dream
twitching in your skull.

No Account
(for D.T.)

I was 14-year-old skittish
when I met my first real boyfriend,
his hair the colour of winter sun,
gaze a slap of sky.
Excuse me—that polite.

He still calls after 30 years,
10 or 20 towns, a spouse or 3
between us. We provide each other
with proof of an earlier existence, validate
stale anecdotes, justify left-over fears—
       sneaking out my bedroom window
       his motorcycle-speed-beer-hands
       smashing three dimensions
       down behind the Legion
           drunk dancing
              dodging the cops.

We didn't know about plans, probabilities,
risk factors, didn't give a shit.
Discipline was a word that fit our mouths
like a bit. We bit, spit, ran
       blinkered into spontaneous combustion
         that burnt through all the after-years—

            my first entrance
            into vast blistered love.

Flash Back

(for L.B.)

Scarlet cashmere sweater, sequin shorts,
you high-stepped through grade five, switch-
blade of a girl with blinding baton and white-tassel boots.
You could hold your breath under water longer
than anyone in our brief world, passed out
in eight feet just to prove it. Tanned
as leather, cart-wheeling down Main Street, sinking
through jittery water, cat fights, lemon gin,
shop-lifting, your dad's gun.
Just as tough as they come, my mom said.
By grade seven, still straight as a sharp stick,
you hung out with boys behind the park hedge,
chain-smoked, cursed, and fucked
through the raw, red night, bragged
you were gonna quit school. Grade nine
cut a fine figure and the shortest,
tightest grad dress in Home Ec history.
Slam of the principal's door, your books flopping
against lockers, butt pitched in the hall
garbage can, clanging
when you left.
                    So what
ever happened to you?
What whippet-bodied boy eating up the track
on sport's day is your kid? Which tattooed girl
pacing the 7-11 parking lot, one eye
full of search, the other blind resignation?
What landlord do you owe two months' rent?
Who's the poor bugger working his ass off
to keep you in smokes and VLTs, the sucker
you will never love no matter what he does,
no matter how hard, how filthy hard
you try?

White Wedding

Resplendent. I was gleaming
bone in a skin of silk. Lustrous,
my aunt's pearls, my smile,
polished manners—
>   *the happiest day of my life.*

Grandmother's anniversary crystal
cut corners on the rented linen cloths,
Mother's garnished turkey, roast beef, glazed ham—
impressive
>   *considering,*
>   the relatives agreed.

They didn't stay for the tossing of the bouquet, wanted
only that snapshot view—
the bride a picture in white,
her white teeth sniping words—

and left before they were wounded.

Child with child

they whispered as I drifted
down city streets, long hair leaf-tangled,
a cradle of heart-beat.
So young! Too soon.

The doctor measured my new boy
against charts and stopwatch:
tick tock too
slow
pursed
lips
rusty wheel ground round our heads.
We dallied home through glittering shop windows—
Turkish delight-yellow truck-shiny bike
and forgot about having his dad's dinner ready for six.

The optometrist checks his watch.
Didn't his mother come?
We're the same size now, my son and I,
and still arrive at the wrong time.
I'm his mother, I say.
So young, he whispers,
drawn back to his boyhood street and that girl
wandering by again as he peers through
his mother's lace curtains,
blinks,
behind his bifocals.

My son smiles, amused,
and finally I am the right age
to be
        flattered
wishing I weren't.

Love Poem
(for Marian)

Two years worth of coffee breaks
I listened to her tell of the boyfriend
who brought her eleven golden roses
every Monday, left love poems
in her mailbox Fridays, but always
spent Sundays with his wife.

Then the Greek lover who lay
beside her for a year, singing of hot seas,
praying for the lamb-flecked meadows
of his mind. He promised

they would run together
under the Grecian sun
even if she had to wear a hat
to protect her pale skin, even
if no children ever stumbled from her womb.
It didn't matter she was older, had been with other men,
married before. He didn't care what the villagers would say,
even if she could not have his children.
He booked passage ahead of her
and she sold her furniture, gave away paintings,
bought a one-way ticket and a second-hand trunk.
Goodbye

she told us all at work. But
no letters patterned with Mediterranean sweat
arrived in the mail, no elongated English vowels
encircling her through phone lines.

She needs her job back
she tells me, lighting a cigarette.
Her face folds like paper. A flame
dissolves her eyes.

Gravity

Red: lips, roses, the flush
at her temple and cheek. She
was the apple of the wedding photographer's eye,
her white dress inviting sugary reflection.
She and her prince—
charming as a paperback romance, believable
as all archetypes—tempted
everyone to tears.

She fit into their new house
as easily as into his arms. They
had good-natured spats in the kitchen,
healthy sex in the bedroom,
candles on the dining-room table.

> He told her about flying
> his plane, the blue prayer of winter sky
> that folded him inside psalms of cloud.
> He'd seen ice crystals seed prisms to enclose him,
> how they made him forget gravity.

That they discovered at the same time.

His coffin reduced and fragmented him—
all those broken bones and commitments.
Alone
      she pressed their wedding photographs
into an album, hovered at the edge, not always
able to pull her way in or out.

Time flies.

Nowadays a mindless job, short haircut,
babysitters, and microwave dinners
save her life daily.
She dates whoever, whenever,
for whatever reason, dreams

she's falling down a well.
Her keyboard fingernails grab
at roots and dirt, snap off.

In the yawn of evening
she reads her baby daughter stories
devoid of princesses who live happily-ever-after
and those new, spunky heroines
who always land on their feet.

Thanksgiving

After the meal we smoke at your kitchen table,
grind cigarettes into ashtrays,
mourn in monotones.
You wonder if you'll ever get your child-support,
the plumbing fixed, kids to the dentist, and
I nod, knowing all too well, too well
your litany of worry,
                                        mine.
This is our tradition—Thanksgiving dinner
painstakingly prepared, quickly devoured,
then the door shut on our squealing children
playing outside. *Haven't they grown!*
You ask if I've ever considered remarrying,
and I shrug, try to tell you about a theory
I'm studying, a paper I'm writing, see
you're not listening.

You lean towards me, eyes knife-narrow.
Across congealing gravy and cold potato
you disclose your evening secret—
needlepoint under the living-room swag lamp—
and I wince to think of stencilled cotton
in the lap of your tight jeans,
                                        fingers darting
between smoke and coloured threads.
          Soothing. But some nights
          I can hardly keep my mind on it,
you admit, and we both fumble
for another cigarette.

A flame cuts between us.

Silent now, we get up to stack dishes,
gather leftovers, wrap brussel sprouts
our kids refused to eat. As we scrape the red wounds
of cranberry sauce from plates, I listen to you half-heartedly
describe the almost-perfect ass you saw
last Friday in the bar. From the corner of my eye,
I see how we still move in unison—

dancers in perfect rhythm
                                        clearing away
remnants bitten off and abandoned.

Three nights of no sleep

thin the skull. Kitchen light radiates
hairline fractures and the movement
of coffee cup to lip splinters bone in brain,
blocks the optic nerve until all I can see
are buzzing molecules. Raucous life
pokes into daylight, blind and unformed.
Tongue loosens the chords
attached to dictionary and etiquette, bellows
                                        dungeon and jungle
through the polite afternoon.

At the grocery store
courteous clerks nod
membranes and blood vessels
trafficking oxygen and carbon dioxide
behind the cash register—

whiskey, Prozac, give me God or anything
that hides the blight and toxins under my fresh-paint shine.
I'm buying the facade—coupons, costumes,
                          smiles, smiles, smiles,
and that superficial sense of purpose
bustling down the aisle
towards me.

Night Driving

Drizzle darkens the asphalt, smears light
around lamp posts like butter. Up
and down the street
car headlights pour
                    milk on a long yawn.

A night like this
bloats the heart with its leaking
valves and vows, washes
up old memory—those street lamps
                    gasping holes through the night—

                              that night,
                              Jerry off the wagon
                              and behind the wheel.
                              His daughter and I stunned
                              against the back seat, sweating
                              hand in hand, lights shrieking

                    Jerry go home! For Christ's sake
                    she's married and you're drunk
                              his wife had yelled.
          So why did she let us drive with him?

                    Jerry ranting
                              For Christ's sake!
                    fishtailed the wrong way down Hastings
                    screeched lane through lane
                    horns honking
                              Go to hell!
                    Traffic lights
          in the back window—
          colours of Lake Louise,
          frogs' eyes slashed and oozing
          red pools on the road we poured down
          rain cold.
                    I turned to the front windshield
          jiving light through light
          Jerry shouting
          about long yellow hair
          about hip sway in dance
                              For Christ's sake!

                          Then
    the oncoming tide of traffic
            split open like that sea in my Sunday-school book,
            horns trumpeting our coming and Jerry
            spouting words of love and anger
            like all wild-eyed prophets
                              the world makes way for.

You who have disappeared

pock my dreams with disease, pound
hope into headache night after day.

Are you stumbling streets wine- and piss-soaked,
filthy, ragged, railing?

We who have given up on you,
who you've given up
because we demanded you
sober up before dropping by,
remember our names when you beg
for money, take a bath
before sleeping in our beds—
want to know where and if
                              you are.

Forgive us our vanities, lists of priorities,
personal hygiene products, credit cards, calendars.
We don't have your addictions to diminish
itch, desire, dark visions, or wincing
guilt. On our desks, living room walls
we continue to frame
facsimiles of ourselves
you disdain, look at them often
to remind us who we are
                              supposed to be.

You've descended
dark alleys and decency, ascended
the egotism of identity—
                    God-like
in your veil of filth.

The Year of the Coyote

Oh their terrible stealth!
Babes have been snatched from campgrounds
while parents gathered firewood,
cooked dinner, slept on either side
wild roses bordering carpets of dream.
These days wherever you look, coyotes
lope a lullaby across the horizon,
teeth clipping clean as needles through cloth.
Oh, their red velvet thirst!

We don't allow our kids out the door
without a dog anymore, keep a .22 handy.
Even mid-day, I take the truck to Hilda's.
Her husband stares out the window
at wheat spilling over the prairie,
wishes to hell it were legal to kill
coyotes, shoot them mid-stride.
How their howls snarl up the combines!
Grain, never priced lower since 1917, overflows
bins, wails through rust holes.

Post Office closed down, we straggle
at Gray's Hardware, talk about bankruptcies,
auctions, dogs killed by coyotes.
A few mate with them, steal home
on a leash of moonlight and treason,
wait.

Sometimes I still dream of you,
of you no longer knowing your own children
playing at the edge of twilight. I try
to call them, try and try, but their names
stick to my tongue, consonants, vowels stillborn
in the gorge of distant hills.
I wake up to coyotes ripping open the dark.
You gone.
The howl remains.

Driving home, Hilda talks
faster and faster down the stuttering gravel road,
says she wants another child
but her husband avoids her. All night long
she hears the pad of his feet down the hallway.
At dawn he slinks to the barn to sleep with the chickens.

                                                   I nod,

in the rear view mirror, catch a shape
skirting the truck.

Dirty Dream

Night after night I dream of you—
young and sharp,
the way you were twenty-odd years ago
                                        at your best
when you weren't drunk, raging, burning
the kids to a birthday party pissed, holes
through chairs, couches, our lives.

Your long black hair, perfect teeth, charm
like diamonds—
(We married with two $26 bands)
                    that dazzling, my glimpse into the future
                                                    shattered
            glass. A splinter of reason poked through:
            Pick up.
            Move on.

And when was it?
At least two years ago,
your son and I found you on the street,
your mouth grimacing recognition,
eyes swimming.
                    That's worse
than any anger—your silent weeping over us,
grime and tear-striped cheeks,
nicotine-stained fingers pawing
sad air and the sun overhead
                        spinning
                                like a new penny.

I wrapped my arms around you and for an instant
loved you
not for what you were or could have been,
did or might have done,
but for the open wound you are

Now, when I imagine you—
balding, bloated, a dull glaze over your eyes,
memory smashed after the mugging—

> you stumbling home from the bar,
> fourteen hours of surgery, didn't know
> anything but your first name

I try to sprinkle my voodoo thoughts of you
with sympathy, but shit!
I'd rather scrub you from my mind.

Yet you return
night after night
young and fresh as maggots,
and rage—that rusty knife
guts me.

Making Tabouli

Up and down your knuckles jerk over
strings of parsley, tomatoes spewing
slippery seeds. You pulverize garlic heads,
squeeze a lemon and push the rind
into my bitter grin.

A rioting pattern
—red, white, green—
cuts across the breadboard.

Onions make me weep, you told me
while making tabouli after your niece's death,
your lost job, the incident with the neighbour girl
and her godfather in the black van.
It's always tabouli—garden vegetables
refined by a knife.

Foreign Homes

The land I love is foreign.
I linger in orchards of figs,
dates, olives, carob.
You pick each fruit, offer them
with words I can't understand
spoken in a familiar voice.
    Khudi habibti
Beneath my lips your heart
explodes, explodes, explodes.

We swim in the Mediterranean,
play Hearts in a bombed-out basement in Beirut.
Down winding roads I lose my way, stumble
on a trail of cigarette burns
partially obscured in black hair.

Now I know
where to find your scars,
give them names and causes—
a chance fall while stealing almonds,
a childhood fight, barbed wire,
half-hearted torture
but you—

                you will not discuss them,
                refuse to heal
                refuse to mourn.

I silently draw you into me,
wash your wounds in cool, clean daylight.

Honeymoon Trip

through the prairies—
his exploration of her life line, her long road home.
This is where I grew up she whispers to a dust-devil
and he rubs his hungry eyes.

After the Saskatchewan border he loses
direction in the spinning heat. She decides
to paint the kitchen that wheat-shade when they return.
There she will dream his hand on the steering wheel
while kneading bread dough, and oh, the sun

glinting off the windshield, how it makes them shine.
Isn't it beautiful, she murmurs, and he squints into vacant horizon.
What? he asks. *Where?*

He can't sleep in the broken-down motel rooms,
stares all night, eyes clotted with space.
Daylight, he steers by her tales of harvest and blizzard,
craves the comfort of a skyline, the certainty of destination,
landmarks, miles. Only when he sleeps
can he position himself in a setting—

salty brown bodies at market,
ageless temples, gardens of fruit.
He hears his name called, his father's name,
his father's father's name, a hand-knotted cord
tying him to place, to assumption—
indisputable he thinks, he thought before
the questions gaping from the huge sky.
Only when he first wakes

can he understand his wife's haggard past.
And so his foot forces the accelerator,
moves the car deeper *Where?*
He wants to return
            to his ignorance
                        of the desolation she's mastered.

Noon light shimmers mirage. He sees himself—
a Phoenician sailor
        driving back, back, back
the prehistoric sea.

Foreign Homes II

With our mismatched glasses dirty
in the dirty sink, we drink wine from the bottle—
               to you, to me, my kids, your new job,
                    to student loans and GST refunds.
If only
I were more skilful and you
less self-conscious, we could cut our feet
free of clumsiness and worn patterns—fly
like drunken angels through this matchbox house.

Through piles of CDs I've promised to order
in the cinderblock bookcase you plan to build,
you search for Chopin.
Come with me you urge into *an overture,*
a rhapsody, at least some concerted effort.
But I yearn for the bite of brazen love
gone wrong, a guitar pulsing
to the artery at your neck.

Every weekend we ponder what to do—
RSP seminars or art films,
the townhouses of your stiff friends,
tumbledown suites of my eccentric ones.
More and more

we stay home.
We fill the rooms with our bodies
more and more.

Habibi I whisper
let's dance.

Eating a Pomegranate in the Bath

Remanie you called it, plucking
it for me, huge in the Co-op produce department,
excessively red. How you cradled it
in your palms, transported to your boyhood
orchard, picking before dawn until
the scorch of noon forced you to sleep
in the shadow of *shummulie* bush.

    Condensation laps the wall,
    sweat on my lips, my teeth
    gouge the peel, rip
    the mouth wider. I suck seeds
    into my swollen belly.

The way you held it is the way you hold me,
ripe fruit easily bruised,
your mouth a prayer.

The New House

Within these walls, you fade.
No longer tall under sky ceilings,
bleached thin by the brilliant south window
you crawl into the smallest room
to sleep away dreams
                    of disappearance.
Vast canvases corner you
in shades of loneliness. You emerge
a stranger.

This house was not your choice.
You wanted only a woman with room
in her womb for your genes to gather.
Her belly is huge. Your mind can't contain it.
One night the moon smashes the skylight.
She screams, curses you, pushes
love from your tongue with a moan.

          Dawn cradles a raw child.
          You hold him, name him yours,
          trumpet the news to neighbours
          you've never met.

All night long you paint the walls of your new house the colour of milk
          to ease the blood and gold in your eyes.

Night Feeding

He cries
and I lift him to an aching breast,
this ball of dough
in the elbow of night.

We fold into the sheets beside you
and the air fills with his scent.
            His chest is rising,
            his silk mouth milky
            and I knead his skin, feather-soft,
            his kiss and prayer skin,
            I need him so much.

We awoke groggy
in a miracle too ordinary to question,
a lump of cells carelessly mixed together
in some dark heat we can't recall.
Your hand, giant against his back,
                        strokes, strokes.
Lately I've noticed how in the shadows
your profile resembles your father's.

Through this night
old with white stars
our new baby suckles.
We touch with fingers
and mouths that spill
and multiply

The Cedar Chest

Today my head's clogged with dull sky, a dime's worth of sun,
and these photographs pulled from the bottom drawer of my dead
ex-mother-in-law's cedar chest. There she is
        young and lipsticked, standing in the sun
        beside her husband, handsome in the military uniform
        that covers his wounds, the black and blue veins
        that ran away with his heart. And there—
        two boys captured mid-grin, mid-wriggle,
        well groomed in every picture
                        scrubbed
                        brushed
                        posed.

Look closer.
shadows crouch in every shot,
spill through eyes, tearing
the paper edges.
The older boy slumps in skates, refusing hockey.
At school concerts, sullen, will not sing.
He squints into the camera
                    anticipating a light exploding—

Twenty years later
drunk at the bar during his own kids' recitals
                    glass breaking—

Badlands: the first day

Hot wind licks
flesh from butte and canyon,
exposes all secrets.
Mud and ironstone strip
to raw nerve
                    glinting creek crawling
                                    down age and thirst
to a lost sea.

Through layers of sandstone,
savage instinct, bones of my giant ancestors
spur and buck. The sky is a skin drum,
your hands thunderclap and heartbeat.
In my womb, fossils of our descendants
                                    dance—
                                            small arrowheads winging
back and forth for blood.

This morning in the hoo-doos we found extinct teeth and skin,
heat cloying as your distant homeland,
the ghosts of meat-eaters glaring over us.
All afternoon we make lingering love.
                            Sun swings
                                    across night and
                                            time and distance
                                                    mean nothing
here.
So we discard road maps, slip watches
into pockets, hide the egg-timer,
imprint this day in sand.

Convergence

The orchard sparks with death, spills
an apple, huge in my hand. Grapes
withered and sweet as autumn love
brush my thigh—everything
                           falls together.

          Last night the ghost of George Ryga
          curled around me as I lay sleepless in his bed.
          This morning—forever darlings—you bloom
          through loneliness.

At the other end of the orchard
a farmer boxes the morning's pick,
loads them grunting onto a flat-bed.
Between my feet, apples rot. In the branches above
they glisten in a ballet of leaves—
                    the absent, dead, living—
                    we all shuffle the same space
                    synchronized in each other's reflection.

When we spoke over the phone
you said you wanted to come live here,
to fill the days with crates of fruit,
prune with your father's hands, gnarled
as they were when you were our youngest son's age.
You want to come here to me
to go back there
to walk forward into fields of flame.

          In the kitchen at Ryga House
          I wash and slice the apple
          fragrant and crisp as orchard air,
          the sheets of George Ryga's bed,
your words on the phone with our children beside you
                           listening to distances converge.

Leaving Home

I wipe our touch
from the walls of this old house.
Gentle I am with scars—
pocks where pictures hung,
skinned knees, that thin white line
down the side of our face.
In our bedroom
you first held your milk-lipped babies,
years later kissed the stitches on my breast,
murmured *It's all right now*, cheeks streaked
like old paint.

     Just a house, just
     wood and nails after all. After

all these years, these attachments:
     door knocker, stained glass, colour
     of December light, tongues of pipe and wire,
     their nocturnal moans. And that sticky imprint
     of a child's face, two hands pressed
     against the livingroom window.

Our children's growth marks the door frame.
The ceiling's smudged with insomnia
where the oldest
          jumped
trying to catch his dreams.
For God's sake
go to sleep!

     I close my eyes on strangers
     who wait on the porch steps
     eager to move into our youth
     and reassemble our bones.

Loose Feathers on Stone
for Shawnandithit

Shawnandithit was the last Beothuk.
Born circa 1801, she died of tuberculosis
at St. John's, Newfoundland in 1829.
The Beothuks, a First Nations tribe of
Newfoundland, were the victims of
European disease and genocide.

Unmarked Grave

There is no stone, no word or prayer to mark
Our fleet lives, our staggering deaths. Everything
We were is buried in silence under dark
White plots. We mourn absences: budding Spring,
Summer seed, forests full of god and meat,
Our bullet and virus bones stripped of light.
Babies suckle, nothing but curse to eat.
Their mouths, hungry for repair, bleeding bite
The soil—stolen—their flesh, futures, rage
Beneath cold contempt and new subdivisions
Of greed. We languish in sorrow and dirt, betrayed.
Stake me with fences, bullshit, provisions
Of guilt, Weed 'n Feed. I am silence crowing,
Broken wing soaring, language beyond their knowing.

Survival:

polish a table
without falling into its grain,
peel a potato, avoiding dank smell
of earth in its cells, its taste
of groundwater and carcass. Never
walk barefoot in the garden. Or
imagine the new moon offering herself
to the dark sky, its invisible heave.
Avoid swallowing seeds whole, cook
all meat, even when mid-winter scab forms
on the sky, the skin. Turn
from voices in the flesh, search
for the starting point of the circle,
count the infinite, order chaos,
go blind to the rut, the strut, the sweat
in the eyes of young men who shuffle at the kitchen door.
Breathe without smelling.
Eat without tasting.
Touch without feeling.
Hunger but refuse to feast.
It's not so hard to stick to the earth.

These clapboard walls, storm windows,
lamps, guns, china, lace
fabricate the half-life of civility,
every moon, every sun—

a number
erased.

Heirlooms

How the glass came to them—imported from England
in great oak and canvas chests—how it held
the English sun, soft as a worn cotton rag
rubbed into the eye. She dusted each piece,
placed them in the kitchen cupboard.

The spring water changed
in those jugs and goblets, tasted
as if drawn from a pond of dead things.
Fruit flies twitched, tadpoles drowned.
Centuries of decay were transported
to her mouth, jeers and pronouncements—
whores, witches, niggers, injuns.

Shawnandithit cupped her hands
under the pump after that,
would not drink from cut glass
that reflected her misery
and shoved it down her throat.

Working for the Peytons

As a child I learned
that some of the birds
pulling shut the autumn sky
would tumble from its weightlessness
into bullet-bite teeth of dogs
and not return with spring.

Like the others captured before me—
Demasduit, Oubee, and the boys they named
Tom June and John August for the time
of year they were found—
I am lost,
shed by all seasons.

In the upstairs bedrooms
I unpack woollen blankets, peer
down the winding staircase to Mrs. Peyton
far below. *No*, I tell her. *From now on
I'll work only on the ground floor,* dizzy
with so much falling.

Sultry summer days, I garden, coerce
the soil to surrender its caressing grasses
and sucking grubs, impose boundaries,
plant an invasion—watercress and English cucumber—
row upon row of betrayal.

This is the last of the harvest
I chop and shred, but the European
vegetables refuse our laws of gravity
and fly from my hands—
too slippery to catch,
escape my mouth—
too full of air to swallow.
The other servants tell me I'm wasting
                                                away.

I fumble with memories, already
a memory, chew legends I heard
lifetimes ago, my entrance into the cavity of tomorrow.

And I long for the quick miracle of bullets.

The blizzard is my name—

I will not answer.
I'll sit here by the cookstove,
feet pushed too close, trying to quench
the burning bark dazzle of unfreezing toes.
I'll stay in this sweating kitchen,
gaze outside glass at my home and try not to hear

its howl feeding me empty, stoking me cold

fingers scratching at the upholstered chair,
pulling at springs. I sip tea from a china cup,
nod sour gratitude at the woman with skin
starting to tear like the paper they hand me to fill

with prophesies of disappearance

I chew on a chocolate biscuit, sweet
lie in my mouth. I will stay
in this house and hide from the ghosts
who beckon me—Shawnandithit—

into the snuffed-out night.

Sentences: at the Culls'

After working five years at the Peytons'
I have learned their ways, their words,
understand sentences.

What shall we do with her?

When I weakened, they moved me to the Culls'
where I sit and sketch my lives for them.
I choose graphite, refuse colours—
yellow, blue, the flowing flowing red.

I draw twelve ghosts on the page—the ones
my sister, mother, and I
left in camp
        starving.
                All around them
                animals ravaged, land devoured
                sickness passed from mouth to mouth
                the new sustenance—a hole
                in the gut, torn tongue—

Let me tell you
about our hunting fences
constructed with just one exit,
killers awaiting their prey,
an ocean of assailants chasing behind.
Their only choice was between slayers.
Our only choice was
                nothing
                    left
                        for me to reveal
        on these vast white sheets. So
        let them find
                my people beneath snow
                my Beothuk husband never-to-be
                babies I will not have
                the winter I become
                      quieter, colder
                      than their disdain

blank pages at the back of the book
they dream in frustrated inks—
New-found-land the title,
a joke, a riddle, and

What shall we do with—
                me: a suspended sentence

She is crying in a corner

of my mind, next to the dirty laundry,
her skin blistered with shower mildew
and smallpox, gaze hardening
with gnawed bread crust and toil.
She is summer wind
sucked into air conditioners,
tree, bird, fox, fish
pushed into parks, zoos, extinction,
                                    a disease cured by death.

She is everything that must be scoured,
cast-out, shelved, and treasured:
kiss goodnight, midnight hunger,
star, promise, stone—
and so small,
just one coal in a pit of ashes
we huddle around, turning
cold.

So small
I can hardly hear her
screams sinking like a scalpel through sense
and absence, but she is with me,
with us all.

Shawnandithit?

Loose Feathers on Stone

White handkerchief to your mouth, Shawnandithit,
white as your mother's fingertips,
that expanding spot on your sister's cheek
the day they came and took you
as you wandered hungry
ribs hooking ice.
White as death.

Who could have imagined you'd be taken
to a house in town with a fire and embroidered linen
to spit into. Who would have thought death was warm
and plump with meat and men who smile
too much, who ask questions with pencils, wanting
you to draw the canoes, the tents, the chasms
dug for winter houses. They ask you to speak
your language so they can study its sound.
How full of holes it is, subterranean tunnels
echo through your failing lungs
(can they hear?)
Blood in your mouth tastes ripe
as a lover, everything
gone.

And so Shawnandithit, with mother and sister dead,
and none of your people left beating against winter,
it is your turn, the last Beothuk—
                              loose feathers on stone.
In the whitemen's steaming kitchen, you falter, look
to the wall, the calendar you can't read, sketch
them stories of marriage ceremonies, hunting
parties, bullets, disease, and your lingering
death.

Coughing blood,
you fly, you plunge
                alone
                      Shawnandithit,
staining the white, white pages.

Burial

No one has said how they dressed
her after death. Did they kindle her bones
with skins of other beings, nourish
her grave with mourning and meat? Perhaps
they merely wrapped her in a night-dress, gauzy
as bandages escaping a clotted wound,
insubstantial as her days among them.

> I'll bet they just sank her
> in that pine box rank
> with their sweat,
> crossed her, buried her.

Yet I believe

> She became winter
> in our snow-blind lives,
> breathing in the world—
> heat, sprout, bee, love,
> blowing out blizzard and frostbite,
> the flickering flame

in our darkness.

> No one thinks of her
> now, didn't
> spend much time thinking of her
> when she was alive

Servant, squaw,
> she hardly shivered in the cold
Did she ever speak?

> She is the silence
> deep in the permafrost
untouched by bursting spring / I try so hard to hear.

Departures

This winter forest
is silent as any settler's bedroom.
Under snow sheets
my captors dream
of complacency and murder.

I flee them on snowshoes, mark
my departure from the page,
striving for just the right sound
    a howl through needles
the right speed
      one quick rotation of treason.

Earth cracks with cold.
My people's voices—acorns frozen within—
whisper through forever-sleep. But I

skate towards some imagined spring
when trespass is unearthed
and hunger feeds on the blade
of my forgiveness.

When eyes will open.

Empty Seas

Everything gone.

Maybe next year, the fishermen say, salt ringing their sight. Maybe
a silver harvest will swell these lean seas. When we are hopeless, a
gull, a dove, an albatross will wheel through deepwater skies—an
omen, a sign of redemption? Dear God, dear God,

I no longer look to the sad horizon. Shawnandithit, since you
died, they have forgotten. I have all but forgotten you. Once I
prayed that you escaped extinction, found a lover, delivered
brown babies—one little, two little, three little—

Mornings I see you sleep on incoming tides, see you wake to
watch the cold shiver of our days. I've seen

that book in the library, your sketches of bridegrooms waiting,
of elders faded grey, children sifting sand, falling through their
futures. I see

the dry-rot boats in harbour, food bank volunteers in the
abandoned cannery, the empty nets, and I want

to tell them all, it's all gone. There will be no more fish, just
scavenger birds slowly starving, an ocean of drought until our
bellies turn together towards a dying star, until we are wise or
sea-changed or

nothing, Shawnandithit,
like you.

The Pleiades

At night I search for them—
six sister stars emerging from blind
of day to watch continents quake, decaying
green teeth. Their hydrogen hearts pour over
the stiffening dance of earth's eternity.

There was a seventh star once,
so legend goes,
a near-sighted sister looked too close,
burned too hot,
                         dropped
                                        dazzling in love.
How she strained through infinity
to touch that mortal body turning
old before her light-year eyes.

Stunning, her plunge,
falling star-
              woman,
like you Shawnandithit,
reduced to dust. Now when I look up

there are just six stars in the sky
and some forgotten story sliding
down the long gullet of night.

Thieves

Clutter:

this room, the never-made bed, books I should read.
On the sill nectarine, dead flowers, pine cones will remind me of here
when I am back there with you, mid-winter barren, furnace humming
under the children's shrieks, our cool words, sighs of fatigue.
I'll use them to hail heat to tulip bulbs frozen in the garden,
frost eating at the window pane,
your mouth.

Crystal Vase

I place a crystal vase
on the table, fill it
with filtered water and exotic stems.
Setting a place for one
I dream of lovers flamboyant
as the purple blooms of wine
staining white linen.
                  Relationships

fizzle to the bottom
of each week, exhausted.
I wrap a cold towel around my rattled head
and drug a migraine into dinner-party plans.
Lists

on monogrammed stationery
materialize as animal prints and polos
at the entertainment centre. Conversation
touches on all the important issues—tech stocks,
interest rates, post-feminist film, power yoga.
I stare outside at stammering city lights, click
manicured nails against my hand-blown goblet.
It isn't

the door closing behind
ex-boyfriends, detached girlfriends
that unsettles me. Or the trail of litter
to be recycled or tossed.
It's the crystal vase, darkening water,
the odour of decay.

The Fly and I

Winter—slouched against my window,
biting off heart beat and sap, sucking
light from the sky to pour over
your glistening skin—I'm fed up
with your greed and beauty.

A fly left over from summer
buzzes through my room, flight
groggy with its own endurance.

Outside degrees slide into negativity.
Nothing left but my empty sleep
and the out-dated fly. Nothing
but evicted seasons. Remember

last summer? Explosions of sun, beds of flowers,
the haemorrhaging moon? Remember heat
as persistent as snow, the buzzing fly,
every beat of my galled heart.

And still it snows. And winter grows fatter,
sleeker. The fly thumps against black-eyed
glass. Words of the LAWD GOD ALMIGHTY shatter
through the clock radio. A jack-rabbit
dodges street-light, miraculously
escapes into the invisible world DEAR GOD
I long for

dream, the snug universe of a moment,
the molecule a galaxy forms, its climate
ripe as forbidden fruit. Fly
us into its slippery arms.

Another Winter Sunday

thin and still
as the sleeping children pressed
into the mattress beside her.
She covered them with the comforter
her mother sent from England, anticipated
the dark crack of spring, weak sunlight
that would kiss their foreheads, nuzzle
their small scalps if they got well again,
when they got well.

In that one industry town, coal dust
darkened the road, the laundry hung out to dry,
her husband's big miner's hands. And
just where was he then, that Canadian
soldier she married, that stranger,
her sick children's father, the one,
the only one she had to depend on.

Once she sang in the London underground,
in hospitals full of maimed young men
                    There'll be bluebirds over
                    The white cliffs of Dover—
while bombs shrieked. Once she was buried
under rubble when her office was hit,
typewriter keys pressed into her forehead, the words
hang on—hang on—clicking through crushed time.
She had dreamed the children she would have,
rosy as apples
                    Tomorrow, just you wait and see

The youngest daughter opens feverish eyes,
watches, hears her mother.

                    Ever after   she'll recall
                    Love and laughter   wingtips gliding
                                through grey shale days.

The Fly and I

ii

Tooth, needle, blizzard, heart
break stone of winter, you've delivered
another day of absence, your depleted
light and underground ghosts.

A moose nuzzles for dead moss
under a scab of snow and the fly
scrapes the window, even her borrowed
time monotonous, the world
one hard surface
after another.
Here's

blood in your eye—sunrise
drips into sunset
and our nights empty
as the grave.

The Fly and I

iii

Today as I opened the door, the fly
almost succumbed to the temptation
of the world on her wings. Winter
can coax a fly with sweet lies, the promise
of heavenly sleep. I wanted to run
into the snow, but the unlaid ovum
in the belly of the fly and I
now speaks for our sluggish brains,
and we remained shut in,
hatching terror, thoughts bloated with longing.

                        Speak to me of other seasons, fly
                                            backwards
                                        to spring,
                                electric storming
                        youth

How worn
my days have become,
faded and toughened by time and use.
How creaking our dance, so clumsy
the music, the band
                    dropping
                        from the stage
                            one by one
                                dry leaves

fall—
        ing winter
            everywhere.
The furnace hums colours
of hell. I turn up the heat

                    a seed stirs in soil.
                    Maggots crawl
                    from eggs held beneath an icy interval
                    of breath. We hold
                    on

diligent our need, the path of our goals
intricate and seductive as webs,
deadly

                The fly's condemned body
                flinches across glass,
                her eyes fragmenting
    dreams   the long hot sun

Driving Through the Mountains

after Christmas.
Chaos holds every muscle taut.
The word *avalanche* whispers
through clogged veins of snow.

We're silent.

The children's eyes hard
black pebbles skip over
the frozen corpse.
We mouth the name of tomorrow, knot
our hands together, rub stiff fingers over
fraying sweater cuffs, will not
                let go.

              Home in my warm bed,
              night heaves me
              awake. Heart pounding
              I wait for the inevitable
              fall.
                    Children's screams
              shatter. Stars pour
              down vivid cheeks, comets shoot through limbs.

I bring them honeyed tea and lullaby, fold
death back onto a remote mountain shelf. I bury
my face in ticklish bellies
springing warm against my cheek
New Year's (a day away)
                    and new years

Elk

i

A surprise of lazy snow on the new grass
confuses seasons. This morning's
crocuses freeze tears across the slain meadow
an elk walks
            swollen and slow
                        seeking
            another generation among the dying.

ii

Green pine needles litter the rusted forest floor
and only a weak exhalation remains of winter.
A finger of snow thins along the northern branch
of the tree the elk probes with her ripe nose.
In her belly river beats into sea. She is
the seed and the husk in one.

iii

Among firewood in my cabin
I've tossed magazines that contain
upbeat articles on menopause and retirement villas.
One says that as we age
we become who we really are—
                        well,
                        what a lie.

All winter long I dream of crones
who awake old and lost in the woods, crusts and ashes
all they have left in their apron pockets, their aprons
all they have left on their bitter bones.
                        And I'm afraid
that I too will one day be exiled
into winter, grow anger into ice at the heart
of the forest, see only in fractures,
tell only the truth.

iv

Evening news—
                                  glimmering ghost-women drift
across the television screen.
They're weeping, shouting. Holding
pictures of dead grandchildren
they march into the future, step
                                         by faltering step.

v

We've all journeyed through another winter
and as I pass the elk I want to join her,
to settle my joints into rust and emerald, break open
and rise up on wobbly legs. I want to walk to the edge
of the forest with its racket of terrible machines,
to look through eyes old as anguish
and taste with a suckling's hunger.

Last Days

Once she turned her fat ass
defiantly to sun's lather, but winter
withers now, skin thinned
yellow crust.
                The dog and I
wander through mildew and decomposed
litter, stink of farm shit and slough.
Splinters of light fester
firefly eggs and dirty dreams
                      open their eyes.
                            Crude beauty
when season eats season—
the old bones of winter
broken by soft green teeth.

November, December, January:

under a tonnage of night
we dreamt down, want
reduced to zero.
Thin February
wedged in our bones.
We forgot how to hope,
forgot
until

                    the world
                        drilled through our eyes
                            and we emerged,
                                every engorged breath
                                    an effect of the light.

June is the month of funerals

this year. Brides who, Junes ago, held bouquets
of roses in trembling hands, watched
petals wilt through kiss and waltz, who,
an anniversary or two later, felt their bellies swell
the days full, tasted salt on their husbands' jaws—
have fallen from the procession
                              weary
                                        into the succulent earth.

This June we buried my mother and my friend,
the month's fecundity obscene and precious
as the comfort we steal from each other's skin
these cool mornings.

We sang for them—
both mothers—choruses disappearing from our lips,
                              ashes to ashes
cards and condolences
burned in the firepit,
old letters, keepsakes, clothes taken
out with the trash.

In the afternoon and late evening while you work or sleep,
I move from room to room, from youth to middle age,
arranging my mother's furniture, china, memory.
She's moved in, this old woman, her scent
in chesterfield and linen. In my secret ears
she whispers
            my big little girl, my long drink of water,
                              stroking a cheek, my life, her words
stitching and unstitching
                        time.

Light pours onto the tomato blossoms,
my sun-brown hand
(small in my mother's strong fingers).
I pick the last of the irises.
Inside, join them with funeral flowers,
hang them to dry in the window.

Summer Solstice

and you sun on water, you
who can't swim. It's the water's depth,
its unravelling surface, the uncertainty
of shade when clouds shift—black then blue,
the sick jostle of cheap-whisky yellow.

Motorboat blades cut the water
    and gasoline patterns,
    dissipates—a long sea snake
            with a mouthful of beautiful pollution
                          sinks.

    Say I love you. Say it again
    with eyes oil-spill slick, this longest
    day long, your mouth wave
    after wave

Badlands: Retrospect

This desert of scars was once an ocean,
a swamp, a graveyard, sand a breath away from being
                                    wind through our fingers.
We parked at the viewpoint, watched
the kids scramble up buttes as crevice hugged mudslide,
coulee grasped lightning, coal burned backwards
to dinosaur pulse and tropical tree sap, your whisper
wet in my ear.

At the campsite the second hand
trailer lurched through fossil and amber
to sweat and a cold beer,
                          a sky clear as infinity.
Our kids returned, time's backbone rearing
around them, and you and I
reborn in wonder, in weariness, fresh with aged love
as new as all their bright weather,
old as earth.

Thank-you Card

To children, man sleeping under blankets
as dawn thumps grey wings—a warning,
a promise, thank-you

air, food, blood, accident of planets
for these luxuries, midnight deep in me.
For friends snoring softly in folds
of once, hope of again, again radiating
through wrinkling time, the threads
drawn between us, their discreet
patterns of need. Thank-you

for the wild flowers I gathered
on prairie carpets yellow summer long,
for the imprint of a hitch-hiker
with rising-moon smile and knife-blade poems
cut into the blur of hot afternoon,
her bright yearning for destination
and a smoke. What to give

in return for mundane miracles?
A kiss, tobacco, prayer to the cycle
of roots, seed, water to the perennial thirst
of soil and soul? Reverence?

Blessed be the great Mother

Earth—and we your children, inconsequential
as ants marching, as locusts
devouring fields of grain.

Migration

On the last day of summer
I lay on the beach reading poetry
while my kids dug subway systems under a sand city
and seagulls took the horizon
in their cold yellow eyes,
blinked it back, a cry
in its sky-blue throat.

We squeezed the whole brown-sugar day
between our toes, walked to the store for ice-cream,
made wishes on grinning sails.

> Ladybugs came,
> clouds, gusts, a squall.

Wind ripped the lake to bandages,
bound winter to my tan. The ladybugs swarmed
towels, books, elbow creases. I grabbed
the beach bag—
> *Kids, time to leave!*

Sun shrieked across the water,
kids scrambling, and ladybugs
bobbing on waves, crushed under knees, frozen
to the seagulls' southern gaze.

Open Windows
(for C.W.)

New schools, clothes, pens and books,
I bolt and whir from one necessity to the next.
Bits of sanity break off, scatter. Identity
is a hood ornament on the old clunker
I'm ready to sell if anyone's buying—
used mother, well-worn woman (rusty writer?)
slow on the uptake, high mileage,
sometimes, a bit of a gas. Exhaust-
ion trails me, blue smoke diffusing the miles gone by

                                              years
                          I've hurried through. Those who stopped
                          to offer direction, fuel, a push,
                          still with me—
                                  all-weather friends.
                          Their voices, memory thin whisper
                          through bleating rush hour.

At work
purr of wonder, wink of insight
nuzzle up against sharp calendar edges, wrinkle
time, de-pleat it—small revolution
            whirling around the second hand
                    books, business babble, and lecture   break
      apart   and I reach   for the creature in the air—a poem
rescues me from file folders, e-mail, tedious
white noise of my life.

                    Dear friend,
                    You have helped me know the world tenderly,
                          eyes closed, epidermis peeled away
                                  its pulse beating.

Thieves

Your brothers' marriages have worn out
over the years, hardly worth the garage sale price
of old organza and tarnished silver plate.
How the years
                    break us
                              down.
Teeth loosen on the bite of fruit weathered
by too many tepid seasons. Fermenting
juices sting the tongue.
Lies and decay.

One day
a husband looks at his bride
across the dinner table, notices grey
roots creeping into Clairol's Autumn Sunset,
thinks about heading east, re-discovering
his brilliant youth in the dull afternoon.
He squints into the future, sees wrinkled skin and swollen joints
pouring a shaky nightcap, pushes his chair back.
His thigh knocks the table and cold tea slops over
a half-eaten meal.
I'm going out, he says.
Don't wait up.
The plate teeters. Things fall
                              apart.

And some days I despise you
for what you said or didn't say. I hate
your stubbornness, lack of social graces,
stumbling dance steps, the burnt-out light
bulbs and dripping taps you persistently
ignore. But when you're gone

I want you back—your chides, half-raw scent lingering
through the pillows. Under layers of habit and dream
we find each other—reckless nights we steal
and vandalize, nights of wine and syrup running
away with ourselves, and the sour times
I turn from you, you from me, vinegar
in our mouths and eyes.
Our bed is a heap of mismatched souvenirs
                              —dark treasure—
in the naked hours
when we're thick as thieves.

Measurements

i

Children measure my reach and length,
depth of sigh and bone. They
have lived in me and parts they shed
have never escaped my body. I'm implanted
with soft moon nails, crumpled snakeskin, under-water wail
love me
love me

Honey bees buzz my breast, a cheek flushed
silk. Blood from the same sea flows
between our boundaries.
leave me

ii

Fall, and the seed flutters off the branch,
weaves firefly. Shoots
reach from the trunk, its comfort
of sap and deep roots. Hard young man
supples the door frame, bends to kiss me.
"How ya doin' Mom? I brought laundry"
home.

iii

A tart rain, and afternoon light flashes
leaf-grins. My daughter laughs
into the phone, "Mom just got a perm—
Lyle Lovett in drag! And dammit to hell
I'm grounded!" Don't
leave me.

iv

I'm late to pick up the boys from school—
my last two—with molasses eyes and dust-devil skin,
aching for muscle, sneer, and guts. Distance uncoils

between us,
my loose flesh rising from a bed in a house
on a shady street, their taut limbs contained
by a wooden desk and peevish control
as they wait
for the afternoon bell.

              Wind snaps the grass back
              and forth. I shiver,
              rub goosebumps on their lengthening arms.

They lean into the sunlight tumbling
through one of the world's many windows.

(for N.H.)
We were full

with blood, seed, babies.
At night dreams fell from our eyes—
ripe plums across milk-coloured pillows.
Washing dishes, changing diapers, catching
a yawn, we'd see them reappear in our hands,
staining them with poetry there was never enough time
to put down. There was never enough
time, sleep, money then. Fatigue drew
premonitions from our flesh, and we examined them
for affliction and miracle, always found them,
always named them, each time, each one
named in love and worry. Lines etched
across our foreheads, at the corners
of our eyes and mouths. We celebrated
with clowns and cake, we devoured, we fed,
rocked appetites to sleep,
ran the world
                around and around, a carousel
of night and day, years and inches
around and around.

Birthdays, the skies shift. One
by one planets
                fall from alignment.
At the planetarium the children squeeze
in front of a dark-lensed telescope to watch a solar eclipse.
In the sudden night, our bones grow cold.
Fingers, pulling at purses in the gift shop, are stiff,
the coins in our palms, frozen moons.
At home the kids stick crooked posters of galaxies
on the walls of rooms that spin at the end
                                of shadowed hallways.
We call them for supper, but they
                        —light-years distant—
don't hear.

They learn at school that the sun is cooling.
Summers they plan vacations away—
first a night at a friend's house, then a week at camp,
a month in another country—somewhere, anywhere
brighter than home.

The house empty, night plummets
                              like an old sheet
from a rusty ironing board. Stars shine on
insomnia eyes, their heat spent
on remote worlds.
          The kids' high school books tell us
          how far away they are,
          how far away we are,
          how long it takes to send light.

You and I, in our separate towns, garden.
We grow trees that inch through space.
The years hurl by but their numbers count
down, and the trees, inch by inch, remember
them in rings of sap and wear
                              around and around.

One night our trees will catch stars
the size of ripe plums in their branches.
As we pluck them, they'll stain the lines of our palms
with their ancient purple light. We'll eat
cold sweet stars till we're full. And this time
we'll taste every bite.

Biography

Joan Crate was born in Yellowknife, N.W.T. She lives in Red Deer, Alberta, where she teaches First Nations literature, children's literature, and creative writing at Red Deer College. Her poetry, fiction, and essays have appeared in a variety of journals and anthologies. Her first book of poems, *Pale as Real Ladies*, was published by Brick Books in 1989, the same year that NeWest Press published her novel *Breathing Water*.